**ILLUSTRATED BY
KIRILL SOKOLOV**

SIMPLE ETIQUETTE IN RUSSIA & THE USSR

By
Irene Slatter

Paul Norbury Publications
Sandgate, Folkestone, Kent, England

SIMPLE ETIQUETTE IN RUSSIA

Paul Norbury Publications
Knoll House, 35 The Crescent, Sandgate, Folkestone,
Kent, England CT20 3EE

First published 1990
© Paul Norbury Publications 1990

All Rights reserved. No part of this publication may be reproduced, stored in a retrieval system, or transmitted in any form or by any means without prior permission from the publishers.

ISBN 0-904404-72-2

British Library Cataloguing in Publication Data
Slatter, Irene, *1942*
  Simple etiquette in Russia. The USSR.
  1. Soviet Union. Etiquette
  I. Title
  305'.0947

  ISBN 0-904404-72-2

Distributed in the USA & Canada by:
THE TALMAN CO. INC
150 Fifth Avenue
New York, NY 10011

Photosetting by Visual Typesetting, Harrow, Middlesex
Printed in England by BPCC Wheatons Ltd, Exeter

Contents

1 *Introduction: A Sense of History* 7

2 Travelling to Russia 11

3 Hotels and Food 15

4 Out and About 18

5 Shopping 21

6 Visiting a Russian Family 26

7 Business in Russia 31

8 General Information 38

9 Useful Words and Phrases 43

10 Useful Addresses and Telephone Numbers 46

1

Introduction:
A Sense of History

Russia is a fascinating place but it is only one part of the Soviet Union which is a vast area — accounting for one-sixth of the world's land surface. Russia, which includes the whole of Siberia, is in fact the largest of the Soviet Union's 15 republics. Each of these republics, involving many different ethnic groups, has its own language and culture. Over 100 languages are spoken within the Soviet Union which has borders stretching from the Baltic to the Pacific, the Arctic and Central Asia.

There are 12 time zones in the Soviet Union and the climate, as one would expect, varies enormously: the northern arctic areas are extremely cold, while in the south, and this includes a great part of the Soviet Union, there is a continental climate with small areas of temperate zones. It goes without saying, therefore, that if you travel to Russia in winter make sure you take a warm coat, warm boots and gloves and a fur hat with protection for your ears. For the other seasons, take the clothes you would normally wear at these times of the year in Western Europe or on the eastern seaboard of the United States.

The Soviet Union came into existence in 1922 after the Bolshevik revolution of November 1917. The revolution came about because of a complex set of circumstances. Briefly, the story up to 1917 is as follows:

In the tenth, eleventh and twelfth centuries the region was divided up into city states dominated by Kiev, of Rus (as Russia used to be known). These states, which were governed according to detailed codes of law, were as sophisticated as those in England and France at that time. Then, in the first half of the thirteenth century the Mongols (or Tartars, as they are sometimes known) occupied Russia - their control lasting roughly two-and-a-half centuries, during which time Russia was cut off from all the cultural events taking place in Europe, including the Renaissance. Even when they had been finally driven out of Russia, the Mongol influence was felt for a very long time afterwards.

With the departure of the Mongols, the city state of Moscow, then known as Moscovy - later Russia - increased its power-base and asserted its authority over the other city states. This was consolidated in the fifteenth century. The creation of what became a centralised state proved to be a very important factor in Russian history. Peter the Great (1689-1725) in an attempt to drag Russia into the 'modern' western world at the time, reformed his court, brought women out of seclusion, started major state enterprises such as shipbuilding, and built St Petersburg (now Leningrad), drawing on the skills and imagination of some of the greatest western architects of the time. Catherine the Great (1762-1796) carried on this policy until the time of the French Revolution (1789) which terrified her so much that she turned her back on western ideas.

It was really only after the Napoleonic Wars (1815) that revolutionary ideas began to grow. But because censorship was so severe, many of the new social and political ideas were forced to find expression in some of the great literary masterpieces of the nineteenth century, for example in works by Pushkin, Lermontov, Turgenev, Tolstoy, Dostoevsky, Chekhov and Gorky. It must be remembered that serfdom, with all its terrible evils, was only abolished in 1861, and although the serfs were politically free, economically their position was intolerable because the redemption payments (which were payments made for the land) were incredibly high, and thus fermented a growing sense of despair right up to the 1917 revolution.

Similarly, the conditions of the urban working class were appalling: these workers were very badly paid, their living conditions were grossly overcrowded, they had, like the peasants, little or no education, and they were exploited by their bosses. With the advent of the First World War (1914) there was a general reconciliation with the government, as happened in other countries, but before long the old pre-war conditions reasserted themselves and the privations, the suffering, the desertion of soldiers in the field because of the war and lack of arms, the famines - all these caused the revolutions of 1917, the first being the Kerensky revolution of February 1917 and then the October Bolshevik revolution. [Note: The calendar was changed after 1917; according to the old calendar the revolution took place in October but now with the new calendar it is celebrated in November.]

Thus, when you go to the Soviet Union and try to understand what is happening today, it is vital to remember her history and the important part it has played and continues to play in the structure and development of modern life.

2

Travelling to Russia (Soviet Union)

The most important requisite (at the moment) for anyone going to Russia (Soviet Union) is a visa. You obtain this by applying to the Soviet Consulate for a form, which can be collected or sent in the mail. The form should be completed with great care and sent back with the required number of passport photographs together with your passport or a photocopy of the first few pages of your passport. The visa itself does not cost very much. It can take as little as a few days to process or as long as four weeks (or even longer).

There are various ways of travelling to Russia. Flying is the obvious way, but if you have more time, it is worth considering a train journey which, say, from The Hook (Holland) to Moscow takes two-and-a-half days. There are also Soviet ships to Leningrad which in Europe leave from Tilbury, Copenhagen, Stockholm or Helsinki; this is a very different sort of journey but one that can be very interesting as well as a good introduction to Russian food.

On arrival in the Soviet Union, the traveller is issued with a customs declaration which should be filled in very carefully. There are questions, for example, on how much money you are bringing into the country, whether you have illegal seeds and plants, guns or drugs on your person and how much jewellery or gold you may have. The declaration is then stamped by a customs official and needs to be kept in a safe place; remember, this form has to tally with the customs declaration filled in on leaving the Soviet Union. The detailed questions found on the declaration form were originally introduced in order to stop the illegal exchanges of money or goods which have been a problem in the past. Today, however, given the fact that travellers are free to use Visa or Access (Mastercharge) cards in any of the foreign currency shops or bars and hotels such questions do not really make sense any more since the visitor can bring in cash and a card and only use the card, therefore bringing out the same amount of money as he or she brought in. In recent years, the use of plastic money by foreigners has been encouraged.

It is also possible that young people travelling to Russia might be asked to produce a certificate declaring them to be free of Aids.

Increasing numbers of people, including tourists, are now visiting the Soviet Union, either in groups (especially as tourists or delegations) or individually if on business. There are also many educational exchanges, where students study in a Russian city for several months.

If you simply want to 'discover' Russia or any of the other Soviet republics, there are various ways to go. You can go as an individual tourist and get a travel agent to book your journey, hotel and itinerary. This is usually a very expensive option. Or, as most people do, you could go as a member of a package group where you pay a lump sum to the travel agent and everything is done for you. This is by far the easiest and most popular way. Young people might like to go to Russia and camp there. This is perfectly possible so long as the journey is worked out in advance and all the places that they would like to visit are stated on the visa declaration.

Sometimes people travelling to Russia may have the impression that once there they will not be allowed to go around on their own. This is far from true: these days visitors are at liberty to break away from their group if they so wish and wander around in the designate towns as they like. It helps of course, if they can read a few words of Russian (see Useful Words and Phrases at the back of this book); on the other hand, many Russians speak English or French or German and usually are very helpful to foreigners. However, it has to be said that visitors are still not free to travel around the Soviet Union at will.

Do not be put off if officials at airports and custom points seem unfriendly. Very often they are no more unfriendly than officials in such jobs everywhere. Individually, the Russian people are by nature very relaxed and welcoming. In fact, it is sometimes said within Russia that the notion of hospitality is a Russian invention!

3

Hotels and Food

Having gone through the various formalities on arrival, you will be taken to your hotel. There are two types of hotel - the new and the old. The new hotels are usually very big and modern and the old ones for example the 'Astoria' and 'Europeiskaya' in Leningrad and the 'National' and the 'Metropole' in Moscow have the most atmosphere and are most central. The accommodation is usually in double rooms - there are single rooms but they are more expensive. With the key you will get a card with your name on it in Russian and your room number. This is to enable you to get in and out of your hotel easily and it should be produced if the person at the hotel entrance asks for it. The card is also helpful to show, for example, to a taxi driver if you do not speak any Russian and are returning to the hotel by yourself.

On each floor of the hotel there is a desk by the lift which is usually occupied by a *dezhurnaya* (a woman who looks after her floor). Their traditional function was to report what was going on but these days, in the spirit of *glasnost*, their function is becoming obsolete and in some hotels these women are being phased out.

All hotels have several restaurants where the food is good and cheap, although the service can be slow (sometimes very slow). It is possible to have a three-course meal with local wine for about 4 roubles (£4 or around US$6.50) per person. Breakfast is usually available in a self-service restaurant (in the hotel) for just over one rouble and is normally very quick. Do try speciality restaurants like those offering traditional Georgian and Armenian food such as chicken dishes and kebabs. There are also some very good Indian restaurants in the main Russian cities.

It is also worth exploring the wide range of Russian food; dishes like Chicken Kiev and Beef Stroganoff (a beef stew with cream) are well known, but there are many other dishes to try like stuffed cabbage leaves, soups such as *borshch*, and lovely salads. When Russians invite guests for a meal the table is usually groaning with food. These days there are a number of fast-food restaurants and pizzerias to choose from; McDonalds have obtained approval to introduce their restaurant chain in the big cities. Coca Cola is also available.

Since the mid-1980s there has been an active campaign against alcohol, which has made it more difficult to buy spirits and wine. The restrictions were introduced because too many work days were lost through alcohol-related problems; furthermore the authorities have been trying to reduce the number of drunks on the streets. Beware of drinking the home-made and very strong *samogon*. On the other hand, do try a drink which is only slightly alcoholic called 'kbass' (*Kbac* in Russian.) This is made from black bread and is very delicious and refreshing especially on a hot summer's day. It can be obtained from tankers parked in busy streets and it is possible to buy a glass literally off the back of a lorry.

An increasingly common sight in the main streets are vending machines dispensing fizzy drinks for a few *kopecks* and ice-cream vendors whose ice-cream is delicious and well worth eating. There are also ice-cream cafes which are very popular and offer a big choice of ice-cream. Some of these cafes which are favourite meeting-places for young people, sell champagne by the glass with the ice-cream; an intriguing mix.

4

Out and About

Transport in the Soviet Union is cheap and efficient. The distances between cities are generally so great that people choose to fly whenever possible. The long-distance trains, however, are reasonably comfortable - especially the softer sleeping accommodation.

The underground (found in all the major cities) generally known as the metro, is easily recognised by the large red letter 'M' outside the station. Russian undergrounds are really beautiful and well worth a visit. The one in Moscow is more ornate than the one in Leningrad but both of them are more like palaces than undergrounds. The trains run every two minutes and are usually quite crowded; whenever necessary, it is the custom to push hard and to be pushed in without ceremony. The travelling public is usually good humoured about this. It costs 5 kopecks (about 5 pence) for a journey, irrespective of the distance. (Using the metro is straightforward and people will normally be only too pleased to help a foreigner.)

Trolley-buses and buses are also widely used and tend to be packed, especially at peak times. The cost of a ticket is 4 kopecks - again irrespective of the distance. Ticket machines are in every bus and everyone pays, no-one cheats and it is not unusual for the money to be passed along the passengers to be put in the machines and then the ticket passed back.

Many of the streets in the big cities are very broad and it can sometimes be quite difficult to cross the road. Crossing places are marked out and it is not unusual for an unwary tourist to suddenly hear a police whistle and then be shouted at by an irate policeman. It has been known for tourists to be fined up to 4 roubles for jay walking.

The Russians are very proud of their cities: like the Metro the streets are clean and there is no graffiti. If a tourist inadvertently drops something, he or she may well receive a tap on the shoulder and be invited to pick up their litter.

There are three types of police in the Soviet Union. The first are the ordinary police in royal blue uniforms. They are armed like most police forces in the West and are involved in the same sort of work, for example traffic problems and criminal investigations. In addition to these are what are called *Druzhinniki*. They are volunteer men and women who wear ordinary clothes but red armbands. They have police powers in that they have the power to detain, they can ask to see papers and passports and they patrol the streets in order to maintain law and order, much like an ordinary policeman. The third group is the K.G.B. and they may be seen at demonstrations but very often are not seen at all. They are not as interested in foreigners now as they used to be and the ordinary tourist or businessman has nothing to fear from them. Furthermore, it is doubtful that every room in every hotel in Russia is bugged (in the past this was assumed to be the case involving many thousands of local K.G.B. 'staff') simply because there are so many foreigners now in the Soviet Union and it is logistically and economically unrealistic to 'monitor' them all.

5

Shopping

Money in the Soviet Union is made up of roubles and kopecks and there are 100 kopecks in a rouble. The official rate for a rouble is currently 10 roubles to the £1 which in turn is based on the value of the dollar. There are plenty of official places to change money. There are also many opportunities for tourists and businessmen and women to change money illegally and get a much better rate - sometimes 10-1. Very often waiters in the hotel or taxi drivers will ask to change money, this is because they can buy goods with foreign currency which are as yet unavailable to the general Russian public. Although this unofficial rate can be very tempting, good sense dictates considerable caution because to do so is against the law, and you could get arrested for speculation. It is also possible that someone could be put there as an agent provocateur. This is most unlikely but it is obviously not worth the risk: the rouble is a non-convertible currency and therefore you are not allowed to take roubles out of the country. You can take out a few coins for souvenirs but the remainder has to be changed back into your own currency at the frontier.

Shopping is very time-consuming because of the endless queuing (line-ups) even for basic goods. The mystery remains how it is that everybody seems to have enough to eat, when there are continuous shortages in the shops. It is interesting to note, by the way, that a string shopping bag (which can be put in a pocket or bag) is called an *avoska* in Russian. This comes from the word 'avos' - meaning on the off-chance. So if people see something they like, they can buy it because they have a bag to put it in. Like the West, Russia has big supermarkets where people go around and put their shopping in a trolley and then pay at the check-out.

More common, however, are smaller food shops. What happens in these is somewhat old-fashioned. You queue at a counter to choose what you want. Then the cheese or sausage or whatever is weighed out and you are told how much it costs. Next, you have to go and pay the money at a cash desk usually in a central position in the shop (where you also have to line up) and you are given a receipt. You take the receipt back to the counter, line up again, give it to the shop assistant and only then do you receive your goods. This is an extremely cumbersome, time-consuming and often debilitating system and the hope is that it will be streamlined sooner rather than later.

One of Moscow's most famous shops is called 'Gum' - situated in the city centre. This is a huge building which is divided up into many little shops by walkways, bridges, fountains and alleys. There are seats and small cafes so it is possible to spend quite a long time there as a considerable variety of goods are on sale, including, for example, traditional Russian hand-painted woodwork which make lovely presents. Many of the modern shopping centres in the West are based on the Gum design. A similar major store in Leningrad is called 'Gostinyii Dvor' and is on Nevskii Prospekt.

There are many interesting and beautiful things to buy in Russia, for example, amber and many semi-precious stones which are made up into rings and earrings. There is an old tradition of wooden goods, vases, spoons, dishes and plates called Khokhloma. There is very beautiful porcelain especially from the famous Lomonosov factory in Leningrad. Books and records are very cheap and for the lover of classical music there is a great wealth of good quality recordings on LP or cassette.

Fur hats have become very expensive and they are now really no cheaper than in the West. There is also a good choice in folk materials such as tablecloths, napkins and wall hangings which are very attractive and of course Georgian tea, in pretty caddies which make welcome presents. For younger children there are appealing, well-made (and safe) wooden toys and for the older child there are slide projectors, musical instruments, stamps and even books in English, German and French.

Attached to or in the big hotels are special hard-currency shops called 'Berioska'. Here it is possible to buy all the articles just mentioned sometimes much cheaper (for pounds, dollars, francs etc.) than in the ordinary shops. A range of other consumer goods that can be purchased for foreign currency are also available in these shops and for this reason, quite understandably, the Russians view these places with a certain amount of envy.

A visit to one of the many Kolkhoz (not state) markets is also worthwhile. Farm workers usually have a small piece of land on which they can grow anything they like and it is this extra produce that they can sell at the Kolkhoz market. The top and bottom price is fixed so the goods can be sold at anything in between and there is a lot of excellent fruit and vegetables to be seen as well as meat and dairy products. It is interesting to note, however, how much more there is on sale at the Kolkhoz markets than at the state shops and of course how much more expensive everything is!

Be prepared for a museum or shop to be suddenly closed for repairs or for what is called 'sanitary day' in which a complete building is closed for cleaning.

6

Visiting a Russian Family

Russian hospitality could well extend to a home visit invitation. However, if this is not offered you should not take offence. It could well be that your Russian friend is simply too embarrassed to take you into his home. It is well known that there is a real shortage of housing in the main cities and much of what there is tends to be concentrated in high-rise apartment blocks and very cramped conditions. Inevitably, young couples are faced with an extremely difficult situation starting off life on their own. The old pre-war communal flats divided out into single rooms are now being phased out. After the war a whole family lived in one such room because accommodation was terribly scarce; now more and more of these flats are being turned over to single people. The kitchen and bathrooms are shared by all tenants. It is planned that by the year 2000 these communal flats will be phased out.

Generally speaking, families have their own self-contained flats even though they are small by western standards. Very often two or three generations share the same flat, which sometimes causes unbearable tensions and is one of the reasons for the high divorce rate (1 in 3 marriages in Russia end in divorce) given the fact that young couples often have no choice but to start their married life living with parents. The average size of a flat is from two to four rooms plus kitchen and bathroom. Top officials and party high-ups have bigger flats with better facilities.

The flats are all built in blocks and usually there are courtyards and play areas where the old people can sit and talk and watch the children playing.

Russian families also go to summer cottages or dachas. These can be rented for the summer or are sometimes privately owned by those who are better off; foreigners are not allowed to rent dachas by themselves. This may change in time.

When you are invited to a Russian home there are a few important rules of etiquette. It is considered very bad form to shake hands over the threshold of the front door. This has its roots in Russian folklore and it is important to shake hands with your host only when inside the flat itself.

For a non-Russian, the question of how to address someone can be quite complicated. After 1917 the Russian words for Mister, Mrs and Miss were abolished. The word *tovarisch* - comrade - is used mainly in political meetings and is not as common as many westerners think.

Strangers, in the street, or underground or bus would use the word *grazhdanin* or *grazhdanka* - citizen or citizeness. When strangers meet or are introduced they will introduce themselves by their Christian names and patronymics (that is taken from the father's Christian name and has a masculine and feminine form) and their surname. Therefore, a man might be called Ivan Petrovich Suslov and a woman - Natasha Petrovna Suslova. Do not be surprised if couples have different surnames. This is very common as women do not take their husband's name automatically and very often retain their own. Children therefore can have two surnames and later choose which one they want.

The Russians shake hands every time they meet an acquaintance. Good men friends will kiss each other on the cheeks three times as will good women friends. Men do not kiss women in public and vice versa unless they are lovers or relatives. Friendship is very openly expressed in Russia as is emotion. It is not uncommon for men to walk arm in arm or hand in hand and this does not mean they are homosexual. They are just expressing the bonds of friendship they feel. Similarly, women will walk arm in arm, as is done in the West, and this is also taken for granted.

It is very important to take presents if you go visiting or simply to give to people you may meet. Russian people are very spontaneous and present-giving is part of their way of life. It is essential, therefore, to make a gift plan before leaving for Russia. The Russians would appreciate pictures of your local or native town, small items of clothing, good soap and books in a foreign language like English or French. For young people cassettes of pop music are very welcome and if you want to be especially generous to someone who has been particularly helpful and kind, you could always present your Walkman as a leaving present; this would be much appreciated!

Whether you go visiting in a private flat or have an official dinner, there will always be toasts and speeches at the table. The meal begins with *zakuski* (hor d'oeuvres), made from various salads, sausages, cold pieces of fish, little pies etc. and usually served with vodka. Vodka is served in tiny glasses and you should drink it down in one go, not sip it. Someone will propose a toast, everyone will drink their vodka and then eat something. On a typical occasion there would be several speeches and many toasts. It goes without saying, therefore, that it is essential to eat the zakuski otherwise the vodka is likely to have a devastating effect!

Typically, the table will be covered with various tasty dishes. It is important to try the food and then to eat a little. If you do not like it, just leave it to one side. Russian champagne might also be served as well as Georgian wine - some of which is very pleasant. After the meal liqueurs would probably be offered like cherry brandy and different types of vodka such as lemon or cherry vodka, Armenian and/or Georgian brandy. People usually remain sitting around the table and go on talking until late into the evening. At the end of the meal tea and coffee are served, usually accompanied by delicious large cakes (*torte*) - often elaborately prepared with cream and chocolate and beautifully decorated.

7

Business in Russia

Business people travelling to the Soviet Union will need an ordinary visa as opposed to a tourist or transit visa. For this you will need the following:-

1. A complete visa application form.

2. Three passport-type photographs (4cm x 4.5cms).

3. A valid passport or a photocopy of the first five pages.

4. A letter from your company explaining the purpose, the itinerary and the organisation you will visit, the length of stay and the flights to be taken.

5. Most important of all, a letter, telex or telegram from the Russians, indicating that they know you and expect you. Without this you will not get your visa.

Transit visas are usually only valid for 24 hours for people travelling via Moscow to Japan or India.

If you wish to start trading in Russia there are two ways to do this. Firstly, you should get in touch with any of the Soviet Foreign Trade Ministries or secondly you should get in touch with the Soviet Trade Mission in Britain, France, America, Australia, or wherever you live. You can only get a business visa through a trade mission or ministry sponsorship. You could exhibit your products at one of the exhibitions in Moscow or elsewhere as these enable the Russians to see foreign equipment and foreign products at first hand. 'Expocentre' is responsible for organising exhibitions; its address is:-

Dom Priuomov, Sokolnichesky Val 1A, Moscow 197113, Tel. 268-70-83 Telex 411185 expo SU.

Soviet Offices work from 9 o'clock to 6 o'clock in the evening, Monday to Friday. Try to arrange your appointments well in advance otherwise you may face delays. The best time to ring top officials is usually between 9 and 10 o'clock in the morning.

It is advisable to send a telex to each organisation you intend to visit, telling them when you will come to see them and what you want to discuss with them - try to include a resumé in Russian - at least two weeks before your departure. The commercial department of your embassy can also follow up these things for you. Nevertheless, it is so much better if you make your own appointments as the Russians prefer this and are therefore more likely to look favourably on you. Most Russian firms have a telex, but not all do. To begin with it might be better if you wrote to the organisation with whom you want to deal. Remember, letters can take up to two weeks to arrive.

Make sure that you have enough business cards with you, one side printed in English and the other in Russian. If your company does not get a reply to its letter it might not mean a negative answer. It could depend on whether or not there is hard currency available for your product. Officials must have detailed information so that they can plan for funds to be allocated several years in advance. You will therefore need a great deal of patience, tolerance and perseverance, but you could be amply rewarded.

Official Holidays in the Soviet Union

New Year's Day	1 January
Woman's Day	8 March
International Labour Days	1 & 2 May
Victory Day	9 May
Constitution Day	7 October
Anniversary of the Russian Revolution	7 & 8 November

If the holiday is on Tuesday the Monday is also a holiday but Saturday becomes a working day. August is the main holiday month so it is better to avoid it. The first two weeks of May and the first two weeks of November can be difficult; evidently, it is best to avoid all these times for appointments.

If you wish to receive letters from your company in the Soviet Union it is advisable to get them sent to the commercial department of your embassy and collect them from there, having first advised your embassy you will be doing so. This is only because you are unlikely to know the name of your hotel before you leave. It is also possible to send urgent mail, including parcels, by courier.

L ocal telephone calls are free from your hotel and you can dial direct from your room. Sometimes you may have to go through the hotel switchboard, in which case just ask for *gorod* (town) and you will get a direct line.

Y ou can telephone from a telephone box for just 2 kopecks. Directories are rarely to be found, but there are service bureaux in all hotels and they will have all the numbers of business organisations, or you can find out at any of the information kiosks in the street. There is direct dialling to most West European countries. You can order an international call from your hotel or make one from the main Moscow post office at 7 Gorky Street. There are operators who speak foreign languages at the international exchange.

If you should suddenly need more money, it is possible to have your currency transferred to the Bank for Economic Affairs (Vnesheconombank - Department of current accounts and transfers.) The telex number of Vnesheconombank is 411174 and the telephone number is Moscow 232-53-00.

There is also an American Express representative at 21a Sadova-Kudrenskaya Ulitsa (Telephone - 254-43-05) who will help you. If you or your firm intend to be in Russia for some time you might want to have a Savings Bank Account which can be used all over the Soviet Union. Again this can be dealt with by the bank for Foreign Affairs in Moscow Vnesheconombank. The exchange of money, purchases and customs for business people are the same as for an ordinary tourist.

You may wish to host a dinner or give a reception. This can be arranged at certain hotels and restaurants including Moscow's Mezhdunarodnaya Hotel. The hotels National and Metropole can be used for small numbers and the Budapest Hotel has a large banqueting hall for big receptions. You could also use the special foreign currency restaurants which will allow you to pay with foreign cash or by credit card. These now exist at the National, Intourist, Kosmos, Metropole and Mezhdunarodnaya Hotels. There are also bars which accept foreign currency.

You can now hire a car with a driver. The charge for a smaller car, such as the Volga, is seven roubles an hour for the first eight hours and then five roubles for each subsequent hour. There is an additional charge if you go over 240 kilometres or if the driver works more than 10 hours. Business people who have an international driving licence (with details in Russian) can hire self-drive Lada cars for 9.40 roubles a day and 10 kopecks for each kilometre, plus the cost of petrol (4 roubles for 10 litres). You will also have to pay insurance. If you want to hire a car it would be a good idea to be familiar with traffic regulations - copies of which are available in various foreign languages. Street maps and plans can be purchased in hotels and bookshops.

The new Soviet leadership under Mr Gorbachev appears to have understood the need for drastic domestic change and has already brought about new economic freedoms which mean that enterprises can take charge of their own affairs, for example, allowing them to manage their own profit. *Perestroika* (reconstruction of the economic system) has changed many things - foreign trade and banking and is encouraging the establishment of enterprises throughout the Soviet Union.

The foreign trade reforms are:-

1. Foreign trade can be organised by more Soviet enterprises. 2. Soviet enterprises will have to have hard currency bank accounts. 3. There is a new ministry to help overseas trade.

ПЕРЕСТРОЙКА

Perestroika

4. There will be more encouragement for exports, marketing and joint ventures.

Joint ventures are now possible (from January 1989) on the basis of 51% Soviet participation and 49% western participation. A lot of control is still left to the individual Soviet ministry.

The Russians are very keen to utilise western know-how especially in the areas in which they are behind. There are some points which are particularly important. It is vital that the joint venture should produce enough money to pay the western partner. It should take the place of a Soviet import; it should show an improved quality and bring new technology into the Soviet Union. There are several areas where joint ventures would be especially welcome: the agro-industrial field; food processing, packaging and distribution; high technology, computers, machine tools, the paper industry, clothes, shoes, tourism and advertising.

8

General Information

ГЛАСНОСТЬ
GLASNOST

Many people have heard the story that there are no plugs in wash-hand basins in Russia. This is perfectly true. The point is, they do not exist - not because there is a shortage, but because the Russians think it is more hygienic to wash under running water. So, if you feel you need a hand-basin plug, buy one that can adapt to different sinks before you leave.

Generally speaking, lavatories in Russia are reasonable. Of course they are perfectly alright in private flats and hotels and they are usually alright in restaurants and public places. However, sometimes it is possible to come across very primitive facilities where there might be just a hole in the ground/or very little privacy.

Sometimes, because of a shortage of toilet-paper, cut-up newspaper is provided as an alternative. If this sort of thing concerns you, carry some toilet paper around with you. Such primitive facilities, however, are far less common today.

In winter especially, it is the custom to leave your coat and heavy boots in a cloakroom whenever you go into a public place e.g. theatre, restaurant or library. An attendant in the cloakroom will give you a ticket to collect them when you leave. It is not done to sit in a restaurant or theatre in a heavy coat.

To go to the theatre in Russia is a very special occasion and you will see that people dress up as if they were going to a party. The intervals are longer than in the West and people usually leave their seats to go to the buffet for a drink or a bite to eat or simply to stroll around with their friends. The conversation is usually very lively and the theatre is always heavily booked as is the opera and ballet. Your hotel would usually be able to help with tickets. The circus in the Soviet Union is also of a very high standard and well worth a visit.

For Russians, the events of the Second World War still play a very important part. There is scarcely a family that did not lose someone and the history of the war is taught in all schools and therefore everyone knows about it. Leningrad, for example, was under siege for 900 days and there are many reminders of this. On the main street, Nevsky Prospect, there is a notice warning people to walk on that side of the road to avoid the constant bombardment. Under this notice there are always fresh flowers.

In every city there are war cemeteries and memorials which are a very moving sight and it is quite possible that you could be taken to one of these. The cemetery on the outskirts of Leningrad contains more than a million war dead. The average westerner knows little about what Russia went through during the war and therefore gaining some background information before leaving for the Soviet Union would be very worthwhile.

Many parts of Russia were destroyed by the Nazis. However, since the war the Russians have spent a great deal of money and effort in restoring their historical past as you will see if you go to Peter the Great's palace (Petrodrovets) and Catherine the Great's palace

(Paslovsk) - both these are outside Leningrad and are very beautiful and are marvellous examples of restoration skills. Do not be surprised if you see a wedding party in one of these war cemeteries. It is now the custom for a couple just married to go and lay flowers at one of the memorials and remember the dead.

Weddings in Russia are celebrated with a certain amount of ceremony. Since most people want to do something to mark this event, the Russians came up with the idea of wedding palaces where the ceremony is conducted by a registrar but with a show of pomp. The brides usually wear a white dress, there is solemn music, flowers and photographs and the ceremony itself usually takes place in beautiful surroundings.

There are now more working churches than before and people are able to participate in church services if they wish. The restoration of many other churches is underway while relations between the Church and State are improving with several priests as deputies in the new Congress of the Peoples' Deputies.

Medical treatment in the Soviet Union is free. If you are ill while staying at an hotel the management will call a doctor who will treat you in the hotel or if you are seriously ill, will get you into hospital. There are no general practitioners as such but there are general doctors who diagnose the complaint and then pass the patients to specialists, all of whom can be found in polyclinics. If you require a simple medicine it can usually be bought over the counter at a chemist.

On the whole, letters and cards take about ten days to reach West European Countries and two weeks to reach America; it is perfectly possible to receive mail in the Soviet Union if you are there long enough. It is also possible for business people to send telexes or telegrams and of course direct dialling has now arrived in many Soviet cities and you can ring out easily.

Most people are perfectly prepared to talk about life and conditions quite freely now. (This has happened since *glasnost* and *perestroika* were advanced by Mr Gorbachev in the late 1980s.) They are quite happy to discuss difficulties and shortages and make their views very clear. There is criticism everywhere, on television and in the press, and demonstrations, which were previously banned, now take place and in some areas of the Soviet Union, like the Baltic Republics, there are opposition parties which have developed quite a strong voice. The political scene has become both increasingly interesting and worrying as the Russian people learn to exercise their democratic rights.

9

Useful Words and Phrases

THE ALPHABET

The Alphabet can be divided into 3 groups to make it easier to learn.

1. *Those letters that look like English and have English sounds.*

А а	a	b**u**ck
К к	k	**k**ite
О о	o	c**o**t
М м	m	**m**other

2. *Those letters which have English sounds, but look different.*

Б б	b	**b**rother
В в	v	**v**est
Г г	g	**g**ate
Д д	d	**d**oor
Е е	ye	**y**et
Л л	l	**L**ondon
З з	z	sei**z**e
И и	ee	f**ee**t
Н н	n	**n**ormal
П п	p	**p**aper
Р р	r	**r**adio
С с	s	**s**tove
Т т	t	**t**on
У у	oo	c**oo**l
Ф ф	f	**f**ather
Ч ч	ch	crun**ch**
Ш ш	sh	**sh**abby

3. *Those letters which have Russian sounds and look different.*

Ё ё	yo	**yo**ur
Ж ж	zh	mea**s**ure
Й й	is the **y** in the word to**y**	

Х х	kh/ch	lo**ch**
Ц ц	ts/tz	fi**ts**
Щ щ	shch	fre**sh ch**eese
Ы ы	the nearest is the **i** in the word **i**ll	
Э э	e	as in the word g**e**t
Ю ю	u	**u**niverse
Я я	ya	**y**ard
Ъ ъ	hard sign	
Ь ь	soft sign	

здравствуйте	zdrastvuytye	hello
доброе утро	dobroe ootro	good morning
добрый день	dobrii den	good day
добрый вечер	dobrii vecher	good evening
спокойной ночи	spokoynoi nochi	good night
меня зовут	menya zavoot	my name is
пожалуйста	pozhalyista	please
спасибо	spasibo	thank you
вокзал	vokzal	station
метро	metro	metro/underground
станция (метро)	stantsaiya (metro)	station (underground)
улица	ulitsa	street
проспект	prospekt	avenue
идите	idite	go
стойте	stoite	stop
переход	perekhod	pedestrian crossing
театр	teatr	theatre
кино	kino	cinema
концерт	kontzert	concert
цирк	tzirk	circus
музей	moozey	museum
завод	zavod	factory/plant
магазин	magazin	shop
вход	vkhod	entrance
выход	vikhod	exit
закрыто	zakrito	closed
касса	kassa	cash desk
телефон	telefon	telephone
почта	pochta	post office
банк	bank	bank
ремонт	remont	repairs
справочный стол	spravochnii stol	information desk

театральный стол	teatralnii stol	theatre desk
паспортный стол	pasportnii stol	registration desk
бюро обслуживания	byuro obsluzhibahie	service bureau
сувениры	suveniri	souvenirs
гостиница	gostinitza	hotel
ресторан	restoran	restaurant
кафе	kafe	cafe
буфет	bufyet	buffet
чай с молоком	chai s molokom	tea with milk
чай с лимоном	chai s limonom	tea with lemon
кофе с молоком	kofe s molokom	coffee with milk
черный кофе	chernii kofe	black coffee
вино	vino	wine
пиво	pivo	beer
за ваше здоровье	za vashe zdorovye	to your health/cheers
было очень вкусно	bila ochin fkusno	it was delicious
я не говорю по—русски	ya ne gavaryu pa-russki	I do not speak Russian
аптека	apteka	chemist
больница	bolnitza	hospital
мне надо к врачу	mne nado k vrachoo	I need a doctor
не курить	ne kurit	no smoking
Москва	moskva	Moscow
Ленинград	leningrad	Leningrad
Киев	kiev	Kiev
Рига	riga	Riga
Ереван	yerivan	Erevan
Тбилиси	tbilisi	Tblisi
Таллин	tsallin	Tallinn
сколько стоит	skolko stoit	how much
один рубль	odin rouble	1 rouble
два рубля	dva roublya	2 roubles
три рубля	tri roublya	3 roubles
четыре рубля	chetire roublya	4 roubles
пять рублей	pyat roubley	5 roubles
шесть рублей	shest roubley	6 roubles
семь рублей	sem roubley	7 roubles
восемь рублей	vosem roubley	8 roubles
девять рублей	devyat roubley	9 roubles
десять рублей	desyat roubley	10 roubles
сто	sto	100

10
Useful Addresses and Telephone Numbers

U.S.S.R. Chamber of Commerce
Ulitsa Kuibysheva 6
Moscow 103684
Tel. Moscow 221-08-11

British Chamber of Commerce
World Trade Centre
Office 1904
Krasnopiesnenskaya Nab 12
Moscow 123610
Tel. Moscow 230-23-58

French Soviet Chamber of Commerce
4 Pokrovsky Bulvav, Apt 3
Moscow 101000
Tel. Moscow 207-30-09

Italian Soviet Chamber of Commerce
7 Ulitsa Vesnina
Moscow 121002
Tel. Moscow 241-57-29

Japan-U.S.S.R. Trade Association
1 Mytnaya Ulitsa, 2nd floor
Moscow 117049
Tel. Moscow 237-24-65

U.S.-U.S.S.R. Trade and Economic Council
3 Naberezhanya Shevchenko
Moscow 121248
Tel. Moscow 243-54-70

COMMERCIAL COUNSELLORS AT EMBASSIES

Australian Embassy
13 Kropotkinsky Pereulok
Moscow 119034
Tel. Moscow 246-50-11

British Embassy
Commercial Department
7/4 Kutuzovsky Prospekt
Moscow 121248
Tel. Moscow 241-10-33

French Embassy
Office of Minister-Counsellor
10 Karahsky Pereulok
Moscow 117049
Tel. Moscow 237-86-64

German Embassy
Economic Department
17 Bolshaya Gruzinskaya ulitsa
Moscow 123557
Tel. Moscow 252-55-21

U.S. Embassy
U.S. Commercial Counsellor
Ulitsa Tchaikovskoro 19/21/23
Moscow
Tel. Moscow 451-25-22

Italian Embassy
Trade Promotion Section
12 Krasnopresnenskaya Nab.
Office 1002
Moscow 123610
Tel. Moscow 252-25-60

Japanese Embassy
Economic Department
5a Sobinovsky Pereulok
Moscow 103009
Tel. Moscow 291-85-00

SOVIET MINISTRIES

Ministry of Foreign Affairs
32/34 Smolenskaya Sennaya Pl.
Moscow 121200
Tel. Moscow 244-43-03

State Planning Committee
12 Prospekt Marxa
Moscow K9
Tel. Moscow 292-56-26

Ministry of Foreign Trade
32/34 Smolenskaya Sennaya Pl.
Moscow 121200
Tel. Moscow 244-34-80

State Committee for Science and Technology
11 Ulitsa Gorkovo
Moscow 103905
Tel. Moscow 229-20-00

Ministry for the Automobile Industry
21/5 Ulitsa Kuzentsky Most
Moscow 103895
Tel. Moscow 221-10-03

Ministry of Instrument Making Means of Automation and Control Systems
5 Ulitsa Ogareva
Moscow K9, 103918
Tel. Moscow 220-75-73

Ministry of Building Materials
2-2 Pl. Nogina
Moscow 103713
Tel. Moscow 228-44-82

Ministry of Machine Tools and Cutting Tools
20 Ulitsa Gorkovo
Moscow Centre, GSP-3 103789
Tel. Moscow 209-01-58

USEFUL TELEPHONE NUMBERS FOR TOURISTS

	Telephone
Intourist Head Office	203-69-62
General enquiries	292-26-92
Aeroflot	
International enquiries	156-80-02
Local enquiries	155-09-22
Intourist representative Sheremetievo - 2	578-56-33
Railway enquiries	266-90-00
Arrivals and Departures	266-93-33
Intourist enquiries (in English)	221-45-13
Central Taxi Rank	225-00-00
	227-00-40
Long distance International Calls	8196
Police	02
Telephone enquiries (Moscow area)	09
Correct time	100
Lost Property: in the metro	220-20-85
in a taxi	233-42-85
in a bus/trolleybus	222-87-53